LET THERE BE PEACE ON EARTH AND LET IT BEGIN WITH ME & YOU

LESSONS LEARNED OVER EIGHTY-SIX YEARS…

ROBERT WYNGAERT

Copyright © 2024 by Robert Wyngaert

All rights reserved.

No part of this book may be reproduced in any form or by any electronic or mechanical means, including information storage and retrieval systems, without written permission from the author, except for the use of brief quotations in a book review.

Available formats
Ebook: 978-1-989950-83-8
Large print paperback: 978-1-989950-82-1
Large print hardcover: 978-1-989950-81-4

CONTENTS

To Barbara, my soulmate and the love of my life for sixty-six years.
To my children; Linda, Danny, and Sandra, & my son-in-law, JP.
To my grandchildren; Chelsea, Amanda, Rikki, Steve, Paul, and Eric.
To my great-grandchildren; Harry, Nathan, Zack, Lucas, Milo, Jack, and Leon.

FOREWORD

The reason I am writing this, my third book, is because I had a dream that I might be able to help people by sharing the valuable experience and wisdom I have acquired over my eighty-six years, that made me the man I am today. This is not about fame or financial benefit; I am simply hoping to do my part to leave a better world for my great-grandchildren. To inspire all those who read it to live a better, more meaningful life.

Perhaps my great-grandchildren will someday read the life lessons I strived to pass along to their parents.

After all, experience not shared is lost.

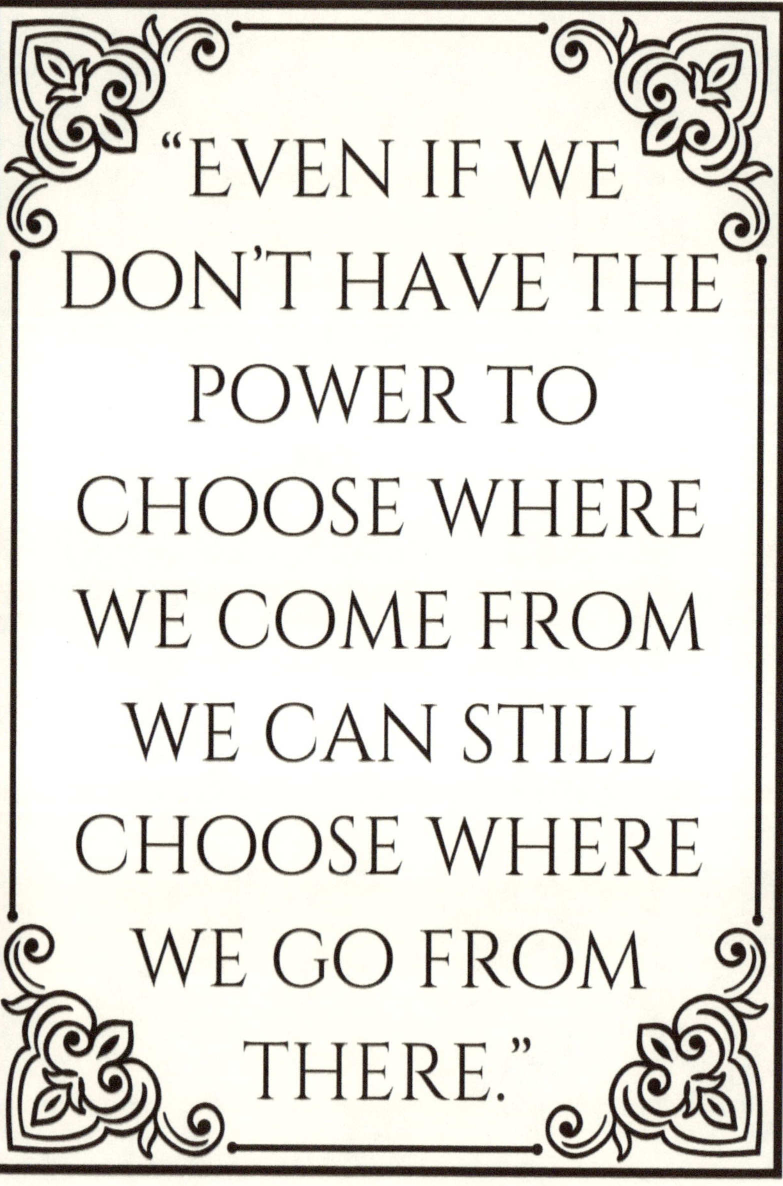

-Stephen Chbosky

WHERE I COME FROM

I am what people call a self-made man. I was born in Montreal, Quebec, in 1938 to Belgian immigrants who worked hard to build a life from nothing but the tiny, abandoned farmhouse they were given. I had very little official education; leaving elementary school to join the work force. I worked my way up through different companies, often holding two full time jobs at once.

I was a gentleman bouncer at Jarry

Park, worked four years at Northern Electric, owned apartment buildings, was a foreman for Canada Packers, owned a restaurant, worked at Pratt & Whitney, and even had a small role in a 1973 thriller movie (The Pyx). I retired from Pratt & Whitney at fifty-five as a Senior Project Manager (and a certified manufacturing engineer), but I started out as a foreman's clerk. And it wasn't so much of a retirement as an opportunity for me to invest my time in a business that was mine, Camping Alouette inc., a campground that I built into a luxury five-star resort over the next thirty years.

My biggest accomplishment, however, is my sixty-six-year marriage to the love of my life, Barbara, with whom I have three children, six grandchildren, and soon-to-be seven great-grandchildren. She was there by my side through failed business attempts, long hours, and now, finally, as we reap the rewards of our labor.

I do not have all the answers. I have failed nearly as often as I have succeeded...but I kept trying. I came from a very poor upbringing, but still managed to succeed in this beautiful country, and to live a life I never could have imagined. Here are the lessons that helped me along the way.

*If you want a detailed account of my life, you can find it in my previous book, Unbelievable but True. If we are acquainted in real life, come see me for a copy of *My Friends Call Me Bob, the extended family version*)*

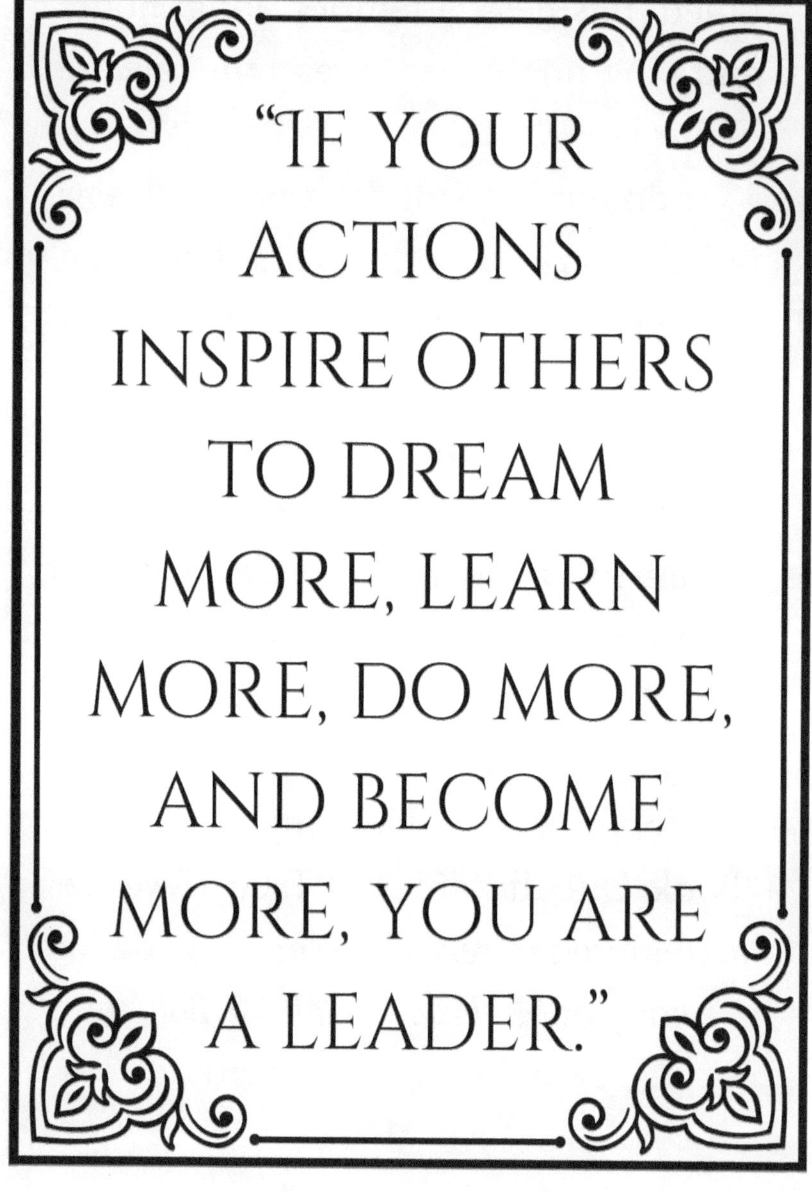

-John Quincy Adams

1

___

TREAT OTHERS HOW YOU WANT TO BE TREATED

This is the core of my book, the main thing I hope you take with you after reading it. There are so many atrocities going on in this world, so much ugliness, that it often feels overwhelming. Even if you are not personally affected, you probably still wonder how you can just sit by and let it happen. What can you do to help? I worry about it all the time. But I also know I don't have the power to snap my fingers and fix everything. What I do have is a wish for peace on this beautiful earth, and the determination that it begin with me. With you who reads this book. With every person who wants to make a difference.

It sounds so simple, so childish and basic, but I believe that the secret lies in loving and being loved. To treat others the way you would like to be treated. That's all we need to do. Because regardless of our beliefs, our religions, where we come from, the color of our skin...at our core we are all human beings worthy of being loved. Of happiness. Of having full bellies and roofs over our heads. Of not being shot in bed, on our way to work, or at school.

I know this is much easier said than done. To replace hate with love? To stop holding grudges in favor of understanding and forgiveness? To not criticize, condemn, or complain about others, but rather praise, compliment, and admire them? In some situations, it seems downright impossible. But there is no future in the past, and you will live a better life with kindness, compassion, love, and a positive mental attitude. Thirty seconds of anger can ruin a lifetime, while a smile can brighten someone's entire day.

I can't suddenly change the world on a global scale, but I can start small and affect change where I am. When I am faced with the option of hating someone who is different from me, I can choose love instead. I can support my neighbors, help strangers, and treat everyone I meet the way I hope someone would treat me (or someone I cared about) if the roles were reversed.

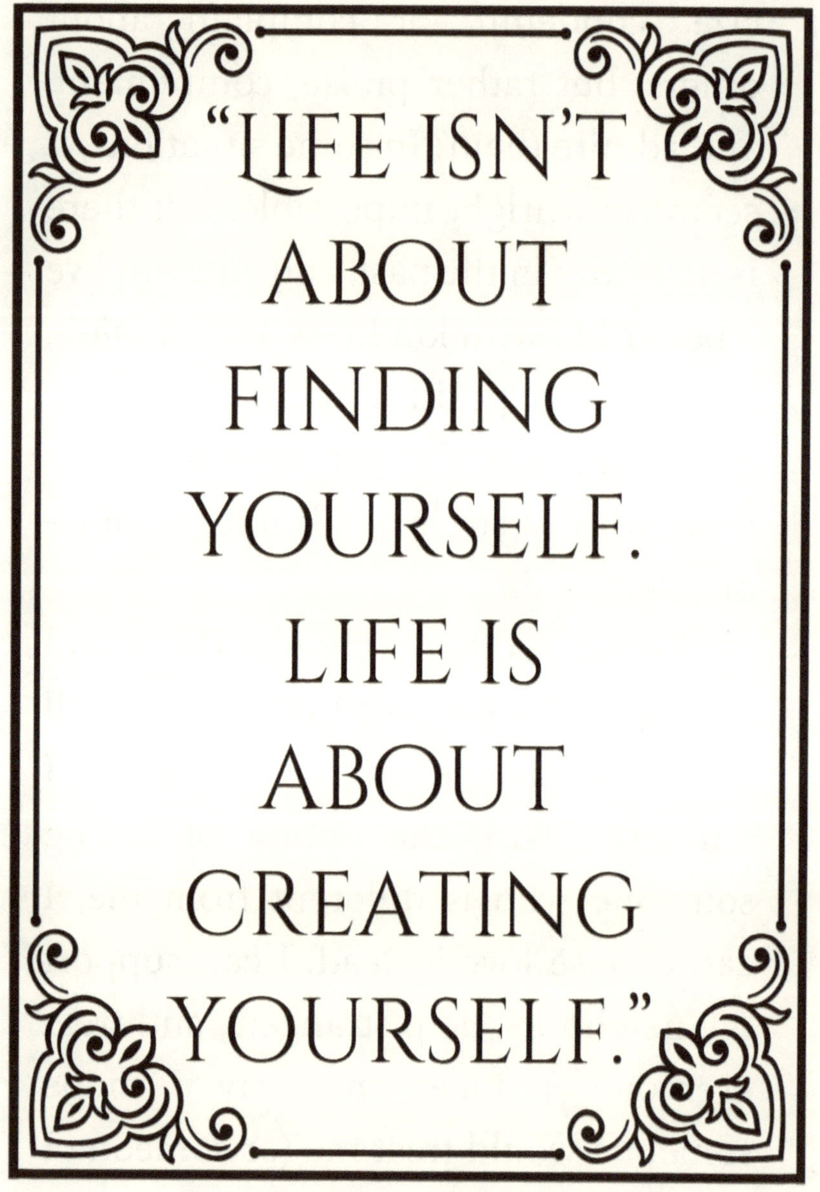

-George Bernard Shaw

2

BUILDING GOOD HABITS

We are all creatures of habit. Barbara and I have been going out for dinner with the same group of family and friends every Tuesday for the past forty years, if not more. But one of the most important habits I have nurtured in my life is a devotion to daily exercise.

When I wake up in the morning, the first thing I do is a thirty-minute routine to loosen and protect my joints and muscles, from my eyes down to my toes. Most of my jobs had a physical element, but I always made an effort to be in shape, so I could protect my family (and others) from harm. I earned an honorary black belt in judo from the YMCA (where I was appointed secretary-treasurer) and attended weekly sessions at Vic Tanny's, as well as the recreation club at Pratt & Whitney. While there, I also helped create a program so everyone could receive self-defence training, if they desired.

One of the easiest ways to stick to an active lifestyle is to get your family and friends involved. It certainly helps to motivate you and, as an added bonus, they can be active and healthy as well. One of my judo exercises was to amble around the house as a duck, to work out different muscles and improve balance, so every weekend the kids would follow me around the house, quacking to turn the exercise into a game. I can't imagine why Barbara never joined in, but at least she was by my side every Friday night, when we booked a local gym to play volleyball with Barb's siblings. Our kids, nieces, and nephews eventually joined in as well.

Since I retired, I have found other hobbies to keep me up and moving, such as golf, gardening, wii golf, and swimming. In 2014, we purchased an endless pool spa, and unless I am in the hospital or there are extenuating circumstances, I do my routine in there every day, rain or shine, summer or winter. Some days are easier than others, but even when it is the last thing I want to do, I still force myself to go out there and do it, because I know it is good for me. Often, I feel better after, and even if I don't, I know my regular exercise is one of the things keeping me alive. And it helps to keep up with the great-grandkids as well!

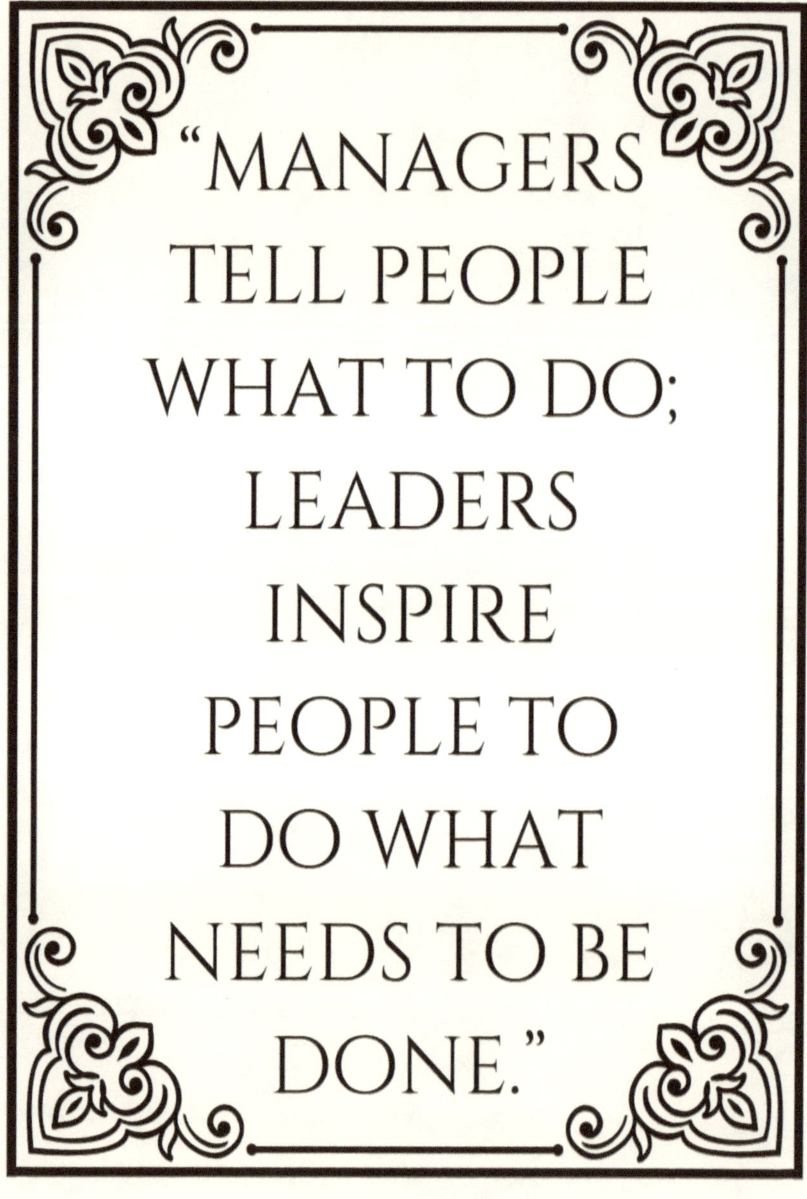

"MANAGERS TELL PEOPLE WHAT TO DO; LEADERS INSPIRE PEOPLE TO DO WHAT NEEDS TO BE DONE."

-Robert Wyngaert

3

WRITING LETTERS

While I was running my campground, we had a folder called 'warm and fuzzy', where we would put any letters or positive reviews. They were useful if you needed a quote for marketing or applying for awards, but they also, as the name implies, made you feel warm and fuzzy after reading them, which is something we all need every once in a while.

I have been keeping letters like that long before I owned the campground. And now, over thirty years after I retired from Pratt & Whitney, I still have the letters and notes I was given when I retired. From the president apologizing for not being able to make it, to my secretaries, who organized my retirement party. I have always strived to treat people the way I want to be treated, no matter their position, beliefs, etc. and it meant the world to me that people noticed, that I had a positive impact on their lives.

Perhaps that is why I have always written letters. I try to catch people doing an excellent job, then I write them letters. These days, they are often of gratitude, to the doctors who keep me alive and spending time with my incredible family, but I used to write a great many letters of recommendation and thanks when people were doing an excellent job, or when they believed in me and helped me achieve my higher potential.

I also write letters when people normally write cards. I like to keep track of all the big events in my life, and in the lives of the people I care about, so every year on their birthdays, my children, grandchildren, and now great-grand-children, receive letters from me. Inside, I remind them of all the positive things they experienced over the past year. I tell them how proud I am of them, how much I love them, how much they mean to me. I share my hopes and dreams for their futures. And I always sign off with 'May God Bless you and Guide You', as well as quotes that have inspired me. I hope they keep them all, so they can one day look back and see all the wonderful things they have accomplished, but also so they know that whether I understood everything they were up to or not, I was always in their corner, cheering them on.

As my grandchildren have been getting married recently, I also write letters for that (as well as births and anniversaries) which include any knowledge or advice I can impart. Not because I believe I know everything, but there were wise men who shared their wisdom with me, and if I don't pass it along, it will be lost.

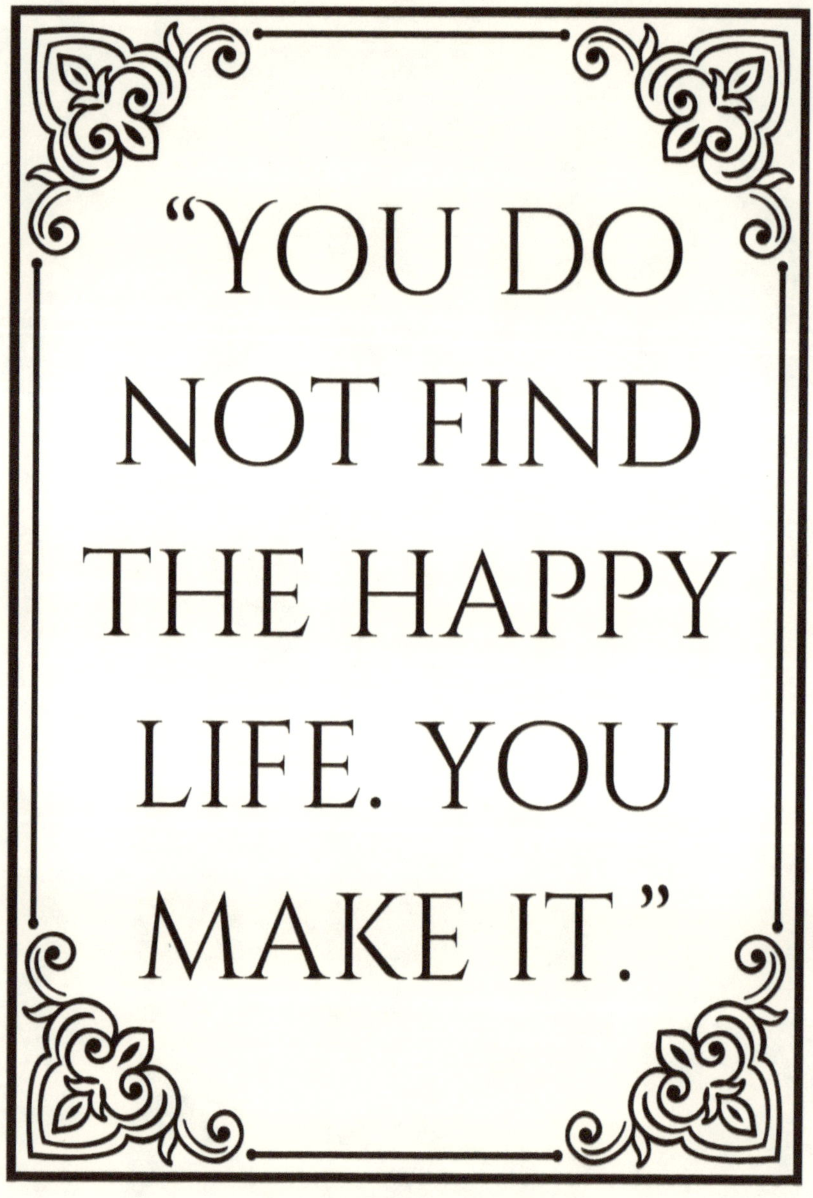

"YOU DO NOT FIND THE HAPPY LIFE. YOU MAKE IT."

-Camilla Eyring Kimball

4

GIVE AN EXTRA 10%

I believe that the people who never do more than they get paid for never get paid for any more than they do. I have always given a little more than I was paid for, because it is that tiny extra that makes the difference. I believe it played a huge part in what made me so successful, because that is what people in positions of power look for when they are promoting people to a higher level of responsibility. As a supervisor, I was always on the lookout for people who were not complacent or mediocre. Who, instead of deciding something couldn't be done, searched for solutions. Who picked up trash when they encountered it on the campground, even if that wasn't in their job description. People who take pride in their work and get it done.

When I worked at Pratt, one of my favorite employees was a sanitary engineer, who was always the first to raise his hand whenever I needed a volunteer. When we met again twenty years later, he was a project manager, because I wasn't the only one impressed by his going above and beyond what was required of him.

I no longer run a business, and I don't have employees under me or a boss to impress, but I still go the extra mile and give an extra ten percent in everything I do. Instead of thirty leg lifts in the pool, I will do thirty-three. If my car is dirty, I will wash it. If there is snow in my driveway, I will shovel it. Even if I have paid a company to do it, or my daughter assured me she will take care of it. It was ingrained in me from a very young age, and I have tried my best to impart it on my children; my oldest daughter who goes above and beyond for her clients (even shoveling the driveway before meeting with an elderly one), my son who always does a little more than I pay him for, and my youngest daughter who kept billy boots in her car when she was a regional campground manager so she was always ready for whatever her people needed from her.

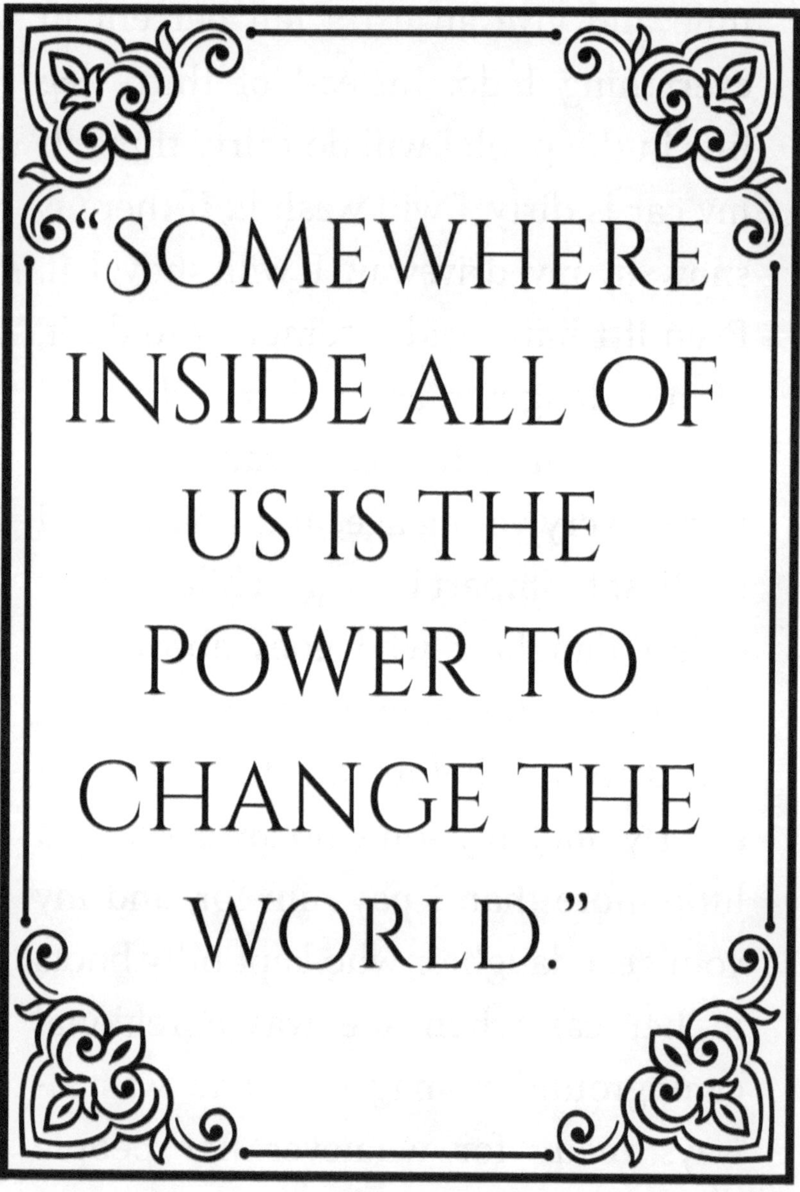

"SOMEWHERE INSIDE ALL OF US IS THE POWER TO CHANGE THE WORLD."
-Roald Dahl

5

YOU CAN'T DO IT ALONE

Everything that I have learned was from someone who had more experience than me.

I had the misfortune of being laid off from my job in the week before my 1958 wedding. I had no clue what I was going to do, or how I would support my family, until my neighbor, Mr. Hancock asked me to help him build a garage for his beautiful car. He had seen me building a house with my father and knew I would be up to the task. When the garage was done, I dug up trenches so he could connect to city water and sewer lines, before his neighbors caught on and hired me as well. Mr. Hancock saw my worth at a time when I was completely discouraged, and kept me going until I was able to find stable, full-time employment.

At Pratt & Whitney, I worked hard for supervisors who saw the potential in me. Who sent me for courses, shared their knowledge, and gave me opportunities to prove myself. Who believed in me.

This in turn led to me becoming a leader who could inspire others. But I wouldn't have been nearly as successful without a great team of engineers, consultants, and contractors working alongside me. I was always on the lookout for people doing a good job so I could have them on my team and nurture them as others had done for me.

Because you can't do it on your own.

Never was this more obvious than when I joined the Knights of Columbus, and incorporated those lessons into my own businesses. The apartment buildings, the restaurant, and finally, the campground. I relied heavily on my wife, my children, family members, former colleagues, and coworkers. We never would have become a five-star RV resort if I hadn't surrounded myself with the best employees, contractors, and vendors I could find.

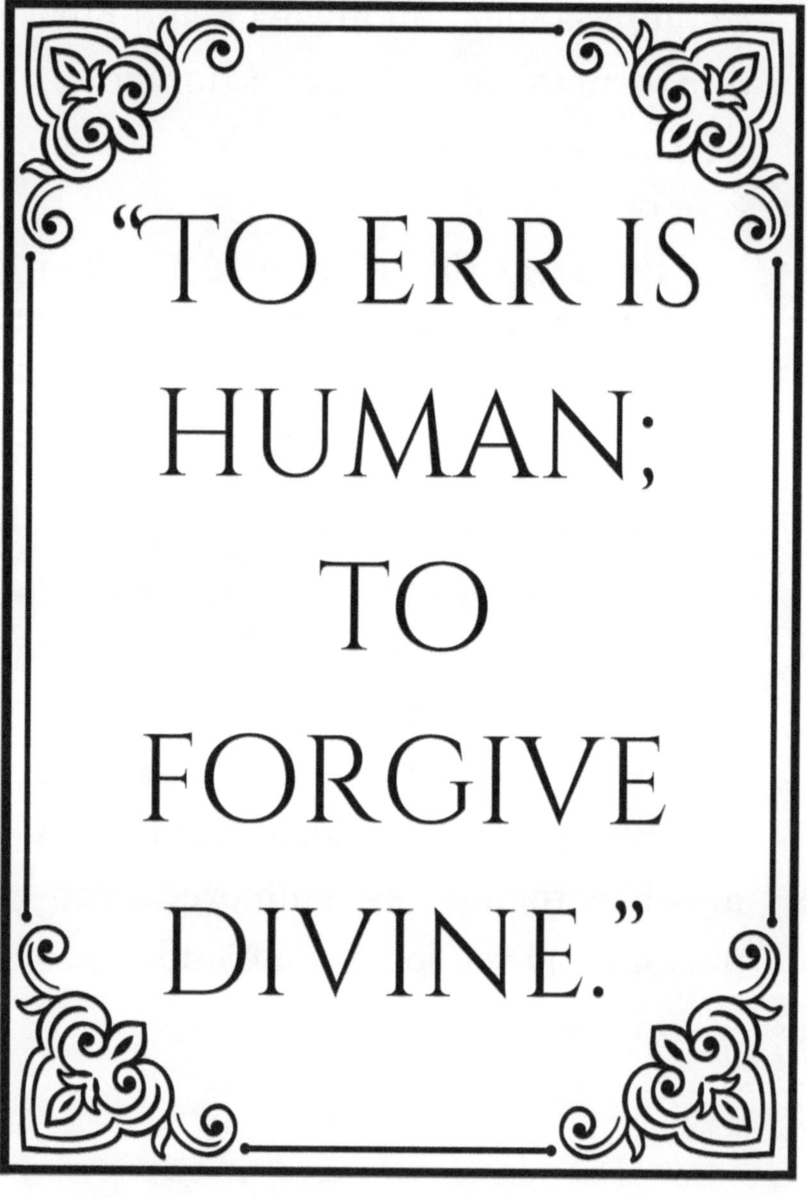

-Alexander Pope

6

FORGIVENESS

Life is short, and is meant to be lived in peace. However, because we are all unique beings with different views and beliefs, there will always be conflicts. On a global scale, between countries, but also on a much smaller scale, within each family and relationship. This is why I believe we must promote more love and forgiveness. Love is something that is not diminished when you share it, it only grows. Forgiving all the wrongs done to you won't undo them, or change the past, but it will surely improve your future. Everyone has experienced hardships in their life, but you can't live in the past. A happy life begins with tranquility of the mind, something that is hard to achieve if you are holding on to hatred, blame, and all the wrongs you have suffered.

It is said that without God's forgiveness, heaven would be empty, and I wholeheartedly agree. Other than babies, I don't know a single person who has never done anything they would need forgiveness for. And I also believe that hating people and holding grudges causes you immeasurable pain and harm, while often doing nothing to the person who harmed you, or to mend the situation. I believe forgiveness is one of the most beautiful things you can do, for those who've hurt you, but more importantly, for yourself. The very important distinction is that forgiving someone does not mean you allow them to keep hurting you without repercussion, or that they have the same access to or relationship with you. It means you've let go of the hatred darkening your heart and are ready to move on. This can sometimes mean resuming your previous relationship, which may be stronger, assuming it was an isolated incident, and the person understands their mistake, but that isn't always the case.

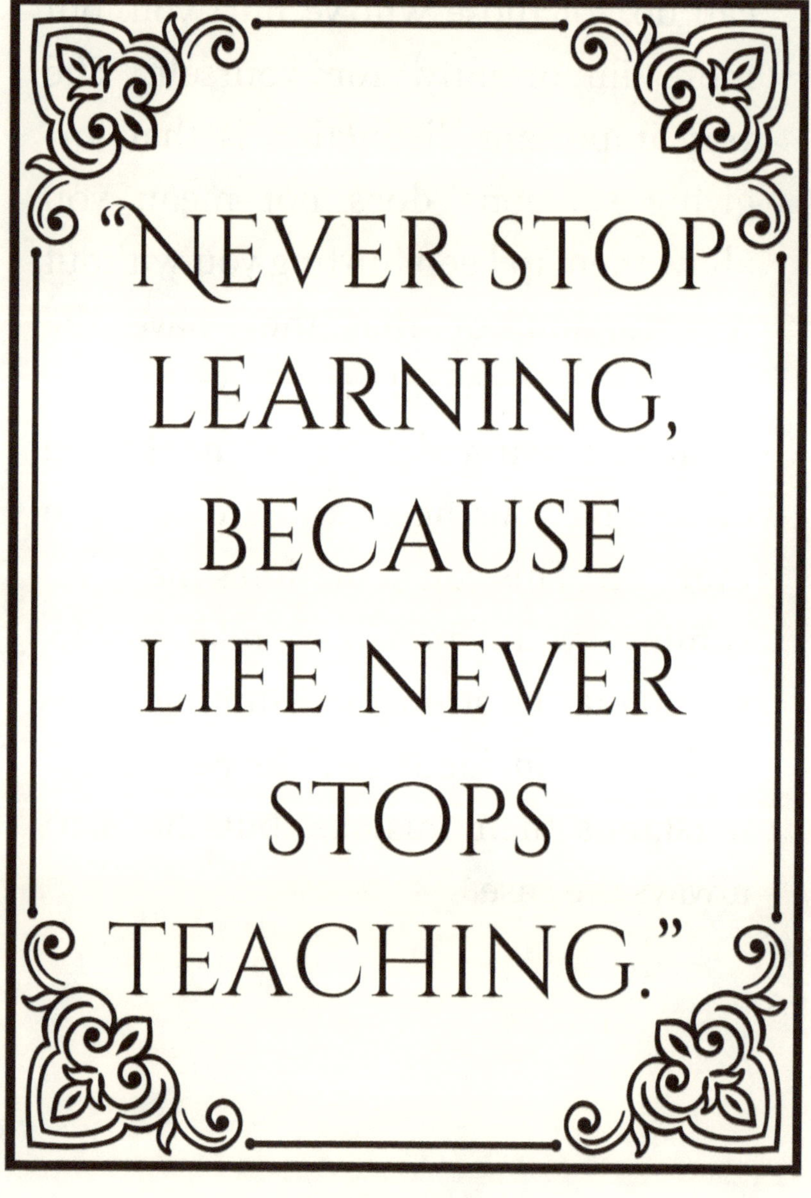

-Lin Pernille

7

ALWAYS BE LEARNING

I can't overstate the value of an education. Coming from someone who left school after the fifth grade to join the workforce, that may sound strange, but I spent the rest of my life making up for that decision. I took correspondence courses to get my high school equivalency and put myself through Dale Carnegie and Toastmaster International when I acquired positions that required more talking (and schmoozing!). Those are the standouts, through which I learnt so much, but looking back, I was always learning. Whenever a course was offered with work, I was always the first to volunteer. Pratt & Whitney even sent me to courses and workshops that were intended for higher management, but while they couldn't be bothered, I was overly enthusiastic. I stood out because I was willing to learn and to improve myself. I know some people who sit through days of training they'll forget immediately after because it comes with a pay raise, but I was never just there to waste time, or because it was required. I listened and learned and went home with binders of knowledge that I actually implemented. I was always trying to find ways to contribute, and learning as much as I could was an excellent way to do that.

When I was running my own business, I was always looking for ways to improve, from our site designs to our customer service...everything. Not just for me, but for my employees as well. There were the standard courses that were required, like how to serve propane or administer first aid, but we also went to all the workshops offered by the Camping associations. Again, some people saw those conventions as an opportunity to party and hang out with old friends, skipping the classes in favor of a paid hotel vacation, but my gang went to every single one, took pages of notes, and tried our best to implement them at the first opportunity. In between the different workshops, instead of huddling together on our own, we spread out and talked to other campground owners, sharing problems, and finding solutions. I also travelled all over Canada and the States with Barbara, mostly to get away from the stress of the campground, but I was always learning. Seeing what my favorite campgrounds had that we didn't, what we could improve, and how we could innovate. Camping Alouette was an early implementer of pull-thru sites and paved roads, and the first in Canada to have an RV Wash and wireless internet throughout the park.

I cannot convey how proud I am of everything we accomplished at Camping Alouette that earned us top rankings across the board. I loved being recognized for all the hard work my entire team put in. But I never hoarded the information. One of my favorite parts of being recognized was having other campground owners visit our site to see how we did it. To be able to share my knowledge and help others improve their business models. It is said that a rising tide lifts all boats, because improving the camping industry as a whole, i.e. making more people want to go camping, helps all campground owners. Just like helping more people live happy and fulfilling lives makes the world a happier and more fulfilled place to live. Knowledge, like love, is one of the magical things that doesn't diminish when it is shared, it only grows.

And when I say always be learning, I don't just mean at work or while you are pursuing particular goals, I mean forever. Even when you are retired and don't see the point in learning new things. It keeps your mind alive and builds connections with the people around you. Every year at Christmas, my granddaughter picks out books she hopes will inspire me and teach me things, which I then pass on to those I feel would enjoy it. This year, I also learnt how to use an Apple watch, because my family likes knowing there are safeguards in place in case I fall while doing all the things they wish I wouldn't do (like trimming down the slope to the riverfront on my property), and I like showing everyone that even at eighty-six, I can still close all my rings! Barbara even learnt how to text message and FaceTime so we can keep in touch with everyone, even while travelling.

The beauty of learning is that it

never stops; there is always something new to discover!

As a bonus, here are some of my favorite nuggets from Dale Carnegie:

Act enthusiastic and you'll be enthusiastic.

Don't criticize, condemn, or complain.

It's nice to be important, but it's more important to be nice.

Anything your mind can conceive and believe can be achieved.

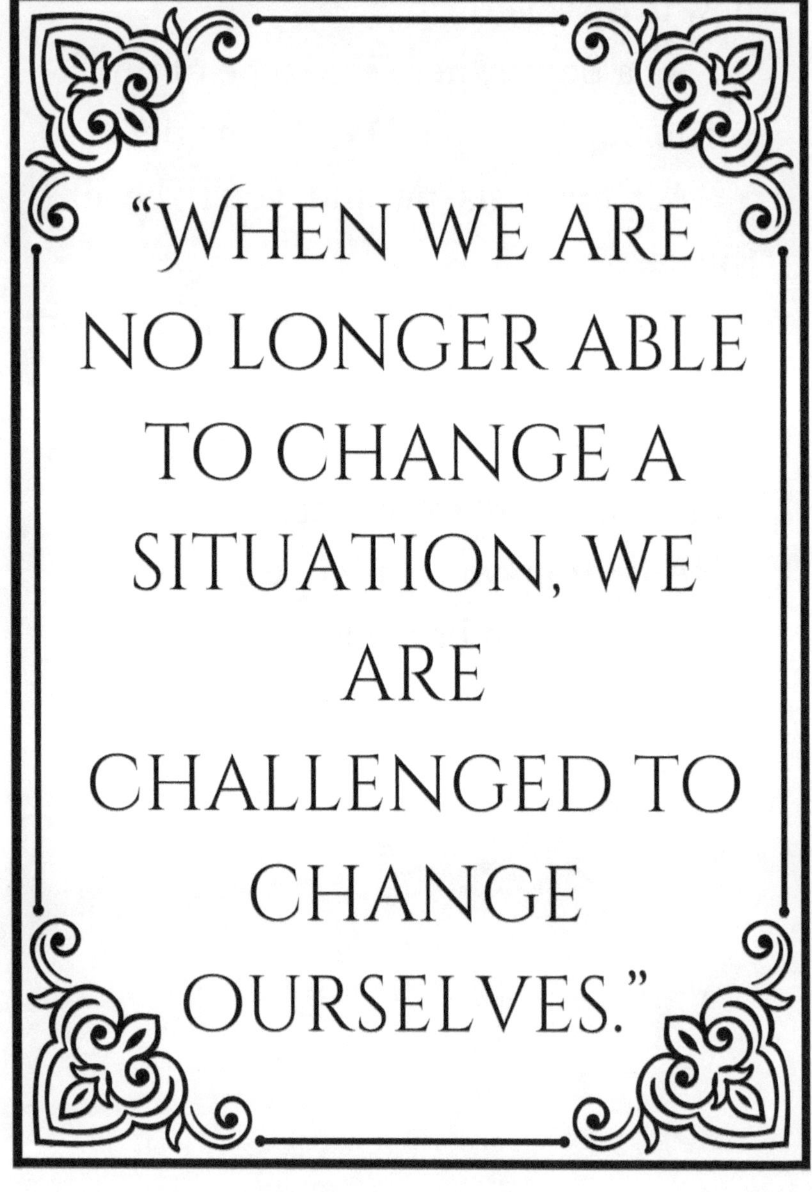

-Viktor E. Frankl

8

YOU CAN ONLY CHANGE YOURSELF

A very hard, but equally important lesson I've learned in my life is that the only person you can change is yourself. We are all individual, unique beings with different thoughts, feelings, and life experiences. You can't force someone to change who they are to better suit who you want or need them to be. Attempting to do so is a recipe for heartache and disaster.

Whenever I forget and try to force someone to be different, or push them to change something about themselves before they are ready (or without considering whether it is actually better for them, or just for me), I like to remind myself of the Serenity Prayer.

"God, grant me the serenity to accept the things I cannot change, the courage to change the things I can, and the wisdom to know the difference."

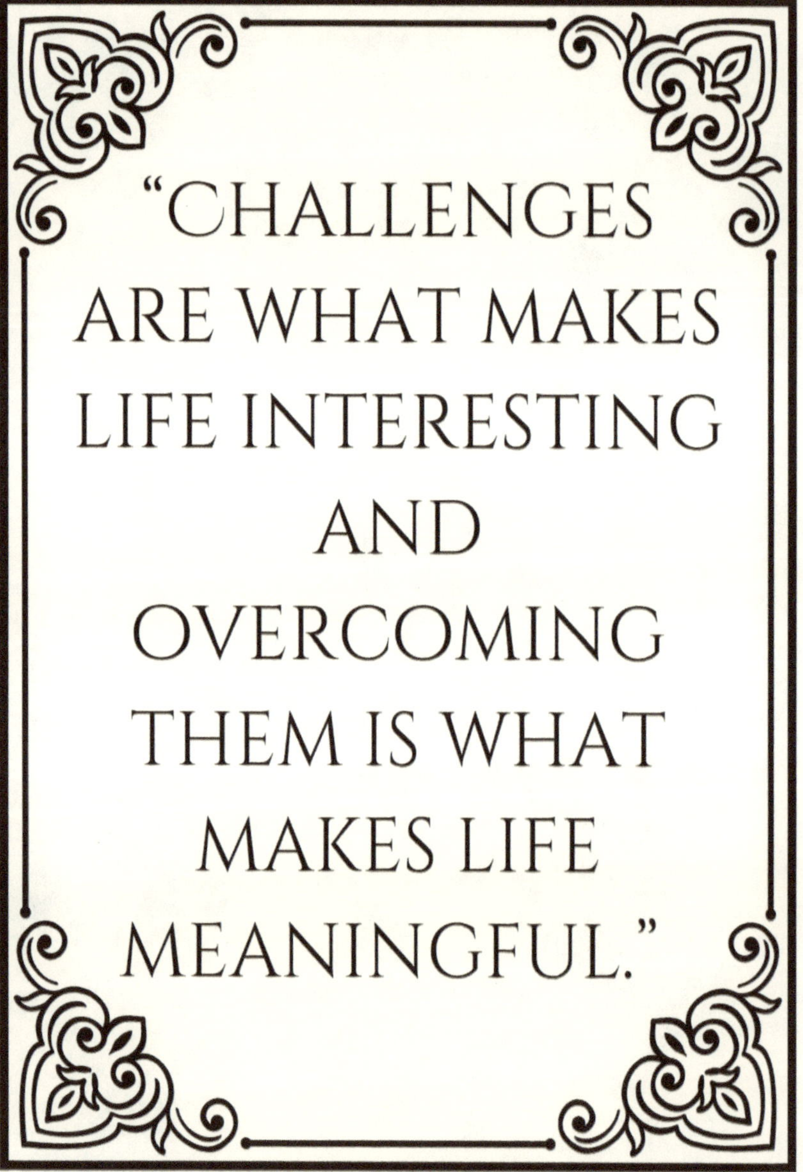

-Joshua J. Marine

9

EXPECT THE UNEXPECTED

In 2020, I got a bleeding ulcer that brought me to the hospital. When they repaired it, they noticed some abnormalities that turned out to be oesophageal cancer. Thankfully, since they discovered it so early, before I had any symptoms, they were able to surgically remove the cancer and twenty-eight radiation therapy sessions ensured it wouldn't come back.

You should know that the procedure during which they discovered my cancer is one where they put a tube down my throat with a camera so they can see inside me. It is excruciating torture, and I have repeatedly told my family that I would rather die than go through it again. But, every three months, I went back to the hospital so they could torture me again, because as much as we like to complain and exaggerate with stuff like that, there are very few things that I would actually rather die than do. These tests were meant to be a precaution, just in case, but for all intents and purposes, I was cancer free. At the beginning of this year, I was asked to come in for another procedure, where they biopsied something that was probably nothing, but again, just in case. When it came back positive, everyone was shocked, including my doctor. Luckily, I always expect the unexpected, so instead of letting this new development tear me down, I had gone in expecting the worst, so I was ready to fight, not give up.

They went in to remove it surgically again, then I was approved for Brachytherapy treatments, where they apply the radiation from inside your body, rather than through the outside. It meant ten more sessions of that torture, but I had an amazing team of nurses and doctors, not to mention my daughter, Sandra, who brought me to the appointments, and I made it through.

Expecting the unexpected is not always about expecting the worst and living your life in fear, assuming death and cancer are lurking around every corner. It is, however, about considering all the options and preparing yourself so they don't knock you too far off course.

Often, it is that fear of the unexpected that stops us from taking the big steps and putting ourselves out there in the world. Because while it can be terrible, it can also be beautiful. One thing I like to do is ask myself what is the worst that can happen? Not to put scary ideas in my head, but to prepare myself. For the endoscopies, the worst that could happen was always that they would discover the cancer was back. Which is terrifying. But thinking of it ahead of time, before it is a reality, allows you to evaluate it calmly and consider your options. How would you react? Because if you are able to find solutions, or be okay with the worst that can happen in a situation, then you know you can handle that situation. You can take that jump.

It is easier as you get older and know what you can handle. When I was younger, I was a bit of a dreamer and sometimes jumped into things without considering all the unexpected that could happen. Like when I opened my restaurant, but a corrupt government inspector delayed my liquor license to the point that I had to sell the beautiful business I built from scratch less than two years after it opened. It was heartbreaking. But, the money from the sale allowed me to purchase Camping Alouette, Inc., which is my most successful enterprise to date, the one that succeeded beyond my wildest dreams, earning every award we set out for...and the one that made my family closer than it had ever been. I do believe that sometimes, God answers our prayers by not giving us what we asked for.

The unexpected isn't always as bad as we think it is. Sometimes the unexpected can be absolutely wonderful, like when it comes in the form of the Cookie Monster showing up at your family's Easter celebration to let you know your seventh great-grandchild is on the way. I was definitely not expecting that!

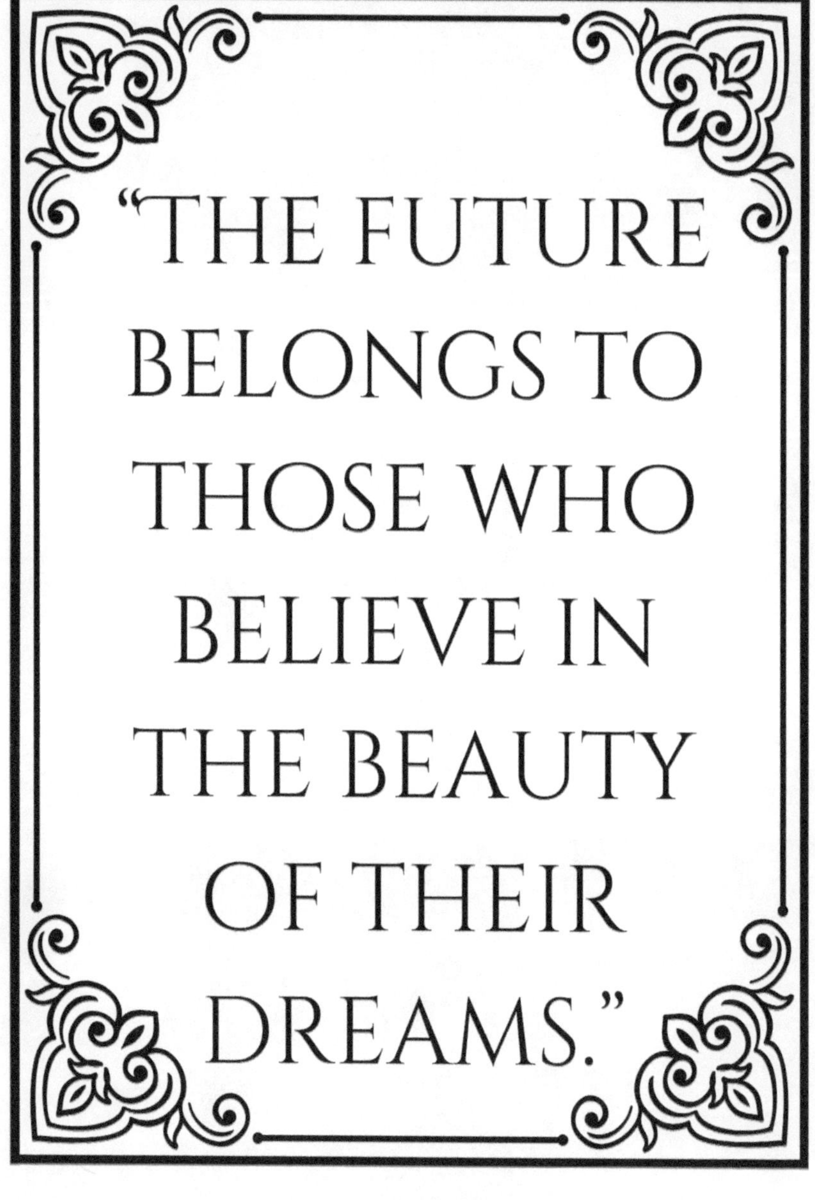

"THE FUTURE BELONGS TO THOSE WHO BELIEVE IN THE BEAUTY OF THEIR DREAMS."
-Eleanor Roosevelt

10

STAND UP FOR WHAT YOU BELIEVE IN

I started out near the bottom at Pratt, and made my way closer to the top than I ever thought I would get, but it was far from easy to get there. I worked hard and earned my experience by working under people smarter than me, making mistakes, and learning from them. I was constantly inspired by my supervisors, and bolstered by the fact that they believed in me. Eventually, I made a name for myself as someone who always finishes his projects on time and under budget, but even that was sometimes a struggle. When I was assigned the dehumidification of one of our plants, with a square-footage of over a million. It was the biggest project I'd ever handled, but they brought me in after the plans had been made by a top consulting firm, and expected me to carry them out as is.

It was costing the company millions to shut down the plant every time the temperature reached 90 degrees Fahrenheit (as per union contracts), so the company was willing to spend fifteen million dollars to fix it...but I wasn't. I was known in the company for submitting the most value control proposals, so as soon as I saw theirs designs, I saw the opportunities to make it better. Or at least more cost effective.

I have noticed that even if a task could take fifteen minutes to do, if you give someone an hour to complete it, most people will take the whole hour. The same goes for money. If you give them a certain budget to accomplish something, most people will use it. I don't know if it is because I grew up fighting for every penny, or because I owned apartment buildings, a restaurant, and a campground with next to no budget, but I always asked myself: How can I do this better? How can I be more efficient? How can this cost less money?

I requested major changes, but my coworkers were not pleased by my initiative, and refused to change anything. I wrote a letter to my superior and explained to him that I couldn't manage the project the way it was designed. He told me this was insubordination, and grounds for dismissal.

I could have shut my mouth then, since I had voiced my reluctance and been turned down. However, my word and my reputation were all I had, and I couldn't put them at stake for a project I didn't think would succeed. So, I wrote another letter, this time outlining my plan, and how it would save the company millions of dollars. I staked my reputation and my livelihood on it, saying they could fire me if I was wrong and implement their original design.

My superior told me I was the most tenacious guy he'd ever met, but the firm of engineers that drafted our current plans didn't trust a man who hadn't even earned a degree in engineering, and the mechanical engineers would not support me if I changed anything.

Again, I could have bowed down and done it their way. But that would have gone against everything I believe in. I may not have gone to school for engineering, but I earned my certification through experience. I started building houses when I was a teenager, and would rather be fired on the spot than put in charge of something I didn't believe in. Which I told the president of the consulting firm, after he reviewed my proposal and tried to convince me to just go along with the original plan. I left our meeting wondering how I was going to tell Barb I'd lost my job, hoping she would understand.

When I got to our next meeting, I found out that not only was I still employed; they'd implemented my proposals! I had to take full responsibility for the project, and accomplish it without the support of the mechanical plant engineering department, but I'd stood up for what I believed in and was able to save the company millions of dollars, cement my reputation, and prove to everyone – including myself – that I was worth betting on.

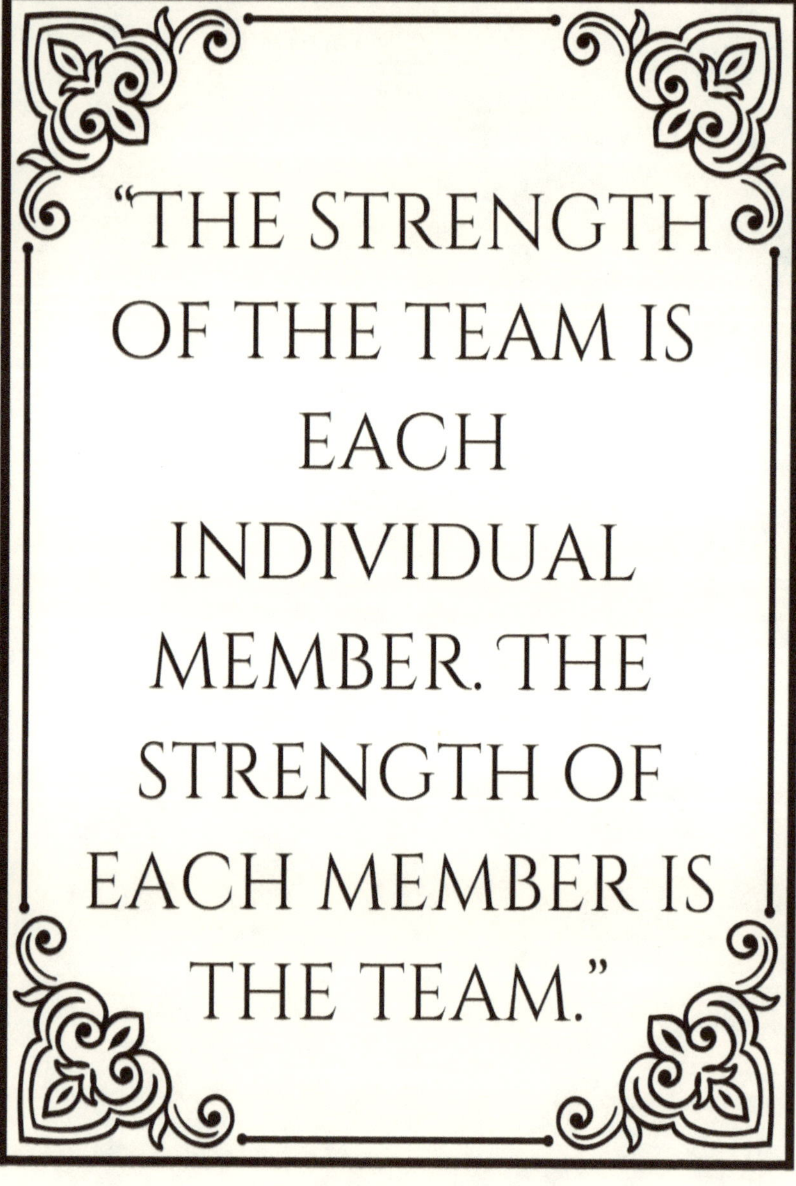

-Phil Jackson

11

ROUND ROBIN MEETINGS

When I was working at Pratt & Whitney, the top senior supervisors, engineers, and architects were required to submit proposals for the projects we wanted to carry out for the upcoming year. These were sent to the financial department to request the appropriation of funds, in order of priority, with budget estimations, start and end dates, etc.

When I was running my business, I did the same thing, only I involved my team in all the decision-making. Every year, we would have a meeting to discuss our most urgent needs for the business to succeed, to be a leader in camping associations, and maintain our five-star ratings. (We were only seven out of 780 other campgrounds) There were the necessary improvements and renovations, but I also encouraged everyone to think out of the box and share ideas for new things we could implement, old projects that could be repurposed...anything they thought might improve our business. We then voted on which projects we would follow through on, and how much money could be allocated to each one. These meetings were incredibly beneficial, not just to make sure everyone is on the same page, but to let everyone's voice be heard, so they all feel like they contributed to the success of the business, because as I often say, I wouldn't have been able to do half the things I've done without the incredible teams I had behind me. I could have simply made all these decisions myself and just told everyone that's what we were doing, but I got ahead in life by listening to the people who were smarter than me, then using that knowledge to come up with ideas and solutions they might not have thought of. Being the president didn't mean I had nothing left to learn, it just meant it was my turn to make the decisions, share my knowledge, nurture the next generation, and be open to new ideas.

You may be reading this chapter and thinking you are not the head of a corporation, so this doesn't apply to you, but I took something I learnt from Pratt and transferred it to what started out as a relatively small family business. And I also used it within my family for non business-related things, like how to spend my bonus, where to go on vacation, and what to name our family dog. There is something magical that happens when people are involved in the decision-making process and have a say in what happens to them. Even if their idea isn't chosen, at least they got to share it, and were shown that their opinions matter; that their ideas have value.

-Kerry Washington

12

DO THE BEST YOU CAN WITH WHAT YOU HAVE WHERE YOU ARE

Growing up, my family didn't have much in the way of money, and I left school long before I had a chance to learn even a quarter of what they could teach me, but I was blessed with the opportunity to learn from those around me. An opportunity I never wasted; from my grandmother showing me how to salvage coal that fell from the boxcars onto the side of the railway tracks, to my father letting me learn how to build a house. One thing I have always had – and heavily relied on – was my family. One of my first jobs was as a clerk in the same field as my older brother, George. He was a customs broker and told me Daniel Kiely Inc. was looking for someone, so I showed up for the interview and was hired on the spot, to my great surprise. Through working there, my boss, Melvin Hedge, introduced me to Barbara, the love of my life. When we were first dating, her father helped me get a job at Northern Electric. And when, just before my wedding, I was laid off from my job, I relied on skills I learnt from my father to support my new family. My father was also the foreman when I started out at Canada Packers.

I am not trying to say that things

were handed to me, far from it, but I would not be where I am today were it not for the people who saw something in me and helped me reach my potential, or the people who taught me the skills to get there.

I never took any of it for granted. I never rested on my laurels, at least not until I could leave my five-star campground in the capable hands of my children (and grandchildren!). I could have gone to Canada Packers and done the bare minimum, letting someone else be in charge. I could have used my father's name to try and get out of things, but instead I took pride in my work and strived to do it to the best of my abilities. To improve those abilities until I could do it even better. I came up with ways to do things more efficiently. I took charge and organized my coworkers to get things done in the limited time we had. It was my work ethic, not my familial connections, that made me become the foreman of twenty-two part-time workers.

At Pratt & Whitney, I was recognized as someone who always came up with ways of saving the company money, but it was often because I just did the best I could with what I had. I knew the skills of the men working with me. I knew which contractors provided the best materials for the best price. I knew what the plants already had, without us needing to spend millions on something new which might cause even more problems in the long run. Basically, I paid attention and used all the tools at my disposal.

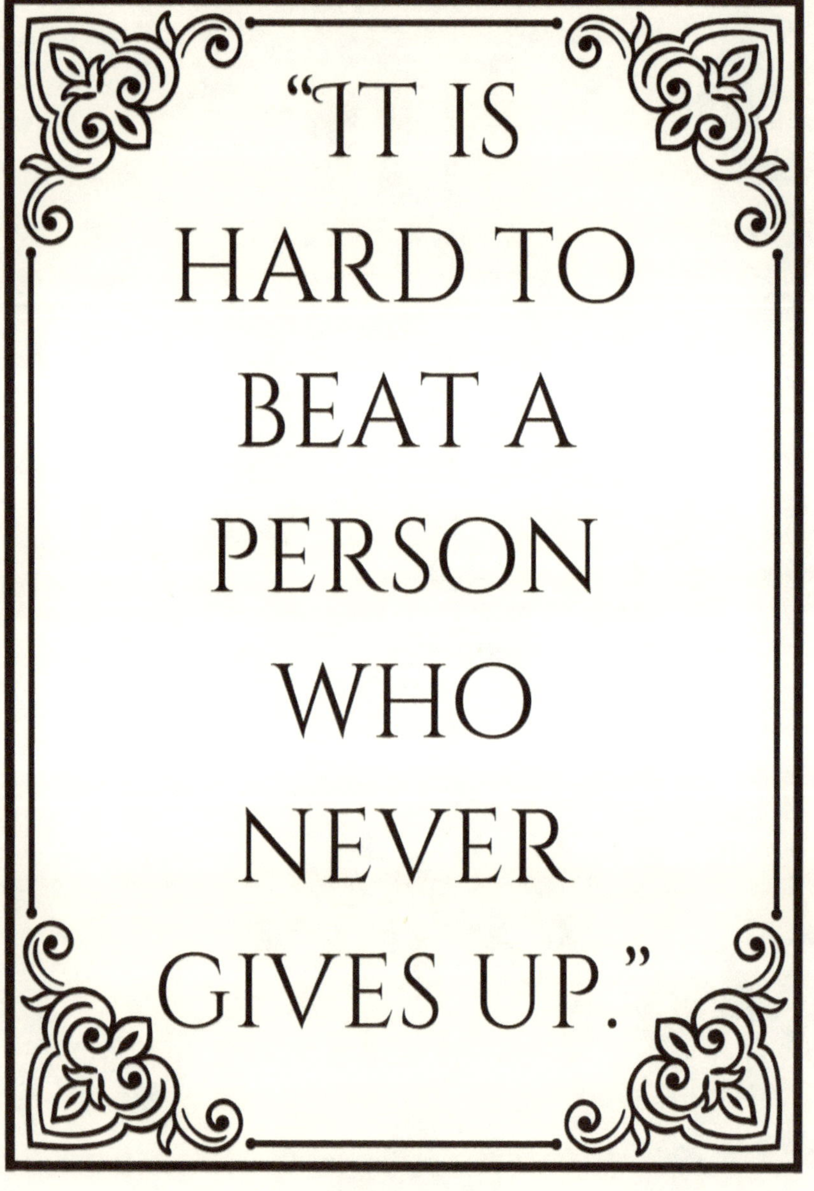

-Babe Ruth

13

———

INVEST IN YOU

This chapter has two meanings. If you've made it this far in the book, you know how strongly I believe that you should always be investing in yourself as far as hard work, education, and never giving up on your dreams. And while I haven't talked much about money, it is definitely a very influential factor in how far you get in life, or at least how hard the journey is.

Barbara and I got married in 1958, in what some would call 'the good ol' days'. Back then the average income was less than 5000$ a year, but you could get a brand new car for 2000$, or have a house built for 12 000$. You could even do your weekly groceries for less than a box of cereal costs you today. Things are getting more expensive every year, and salaries are struggling to keep up with this inflation.

When I started working at Pratt & Whitney, they gave us the option of paying into a retirement fund. I definitely could have used that money and saved myself long hours at my second job, but I chose to invest in myself and my future. To ensure that someday, when I was ready to stop working, I wouldn't have to keep up with having multiple full-time jobs at once, just to keep my family going.

A little over twenty-five years ago, my daughter became a certified financial advisor — the best in the universe, if you ask me — and it renewed my dedication. Not only was she expertly handling my retirement money, I was also able to start savings plans for my grandchildren's education, which gave them a foot up in life once they graduated high school.

I know it is a privilege to be able to put money aside for the future when so many people are barely able to make ends meet as it is. And I am not the financial advisor my daughter is, so I can't tell you what to do, but I can say that if you can afford to put even a little bit of money aside every month, or whenever you can, and keep it invested long term, your future self will thank you. The cost of living keeps going up, and two salaries today are barely able to afford half of what a single salary could back when I got married. The cost of a brand new house back then wouldn't even cover a base model car today. But planning ahead and investing in your future can help soften the blow.

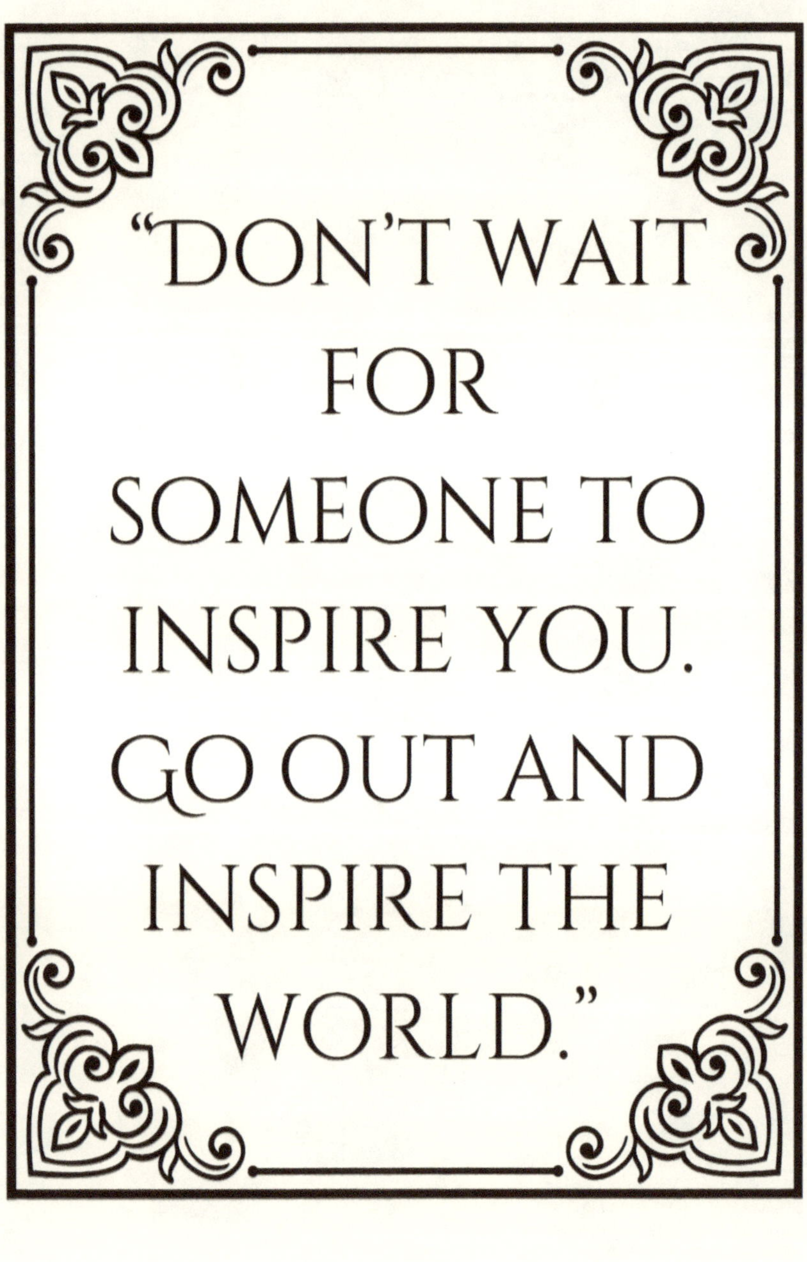

"DON'T WAIT
FOR
SOMEONE TO
INSPIRE YOU.
GO OUT AND
INSPIRE THE
WORLD."

14

THOUGHTS ON GOD

In this perfect world, we live imperfect lives. As children we only learn what our parents and teachers tell us, or show us how to act and behave. However, as adults we are in charge of our own destiny, by the choices we make. Is there heaven and hell? Nobody knows. Let's say heaven is good. Hell is bad. So I believe everyone would like to have heaven on earth, or all that is good.

I believe that being good is easy. But being good all the time is impossible. That is why God said he would have to forgive everyone, or heaven would be empty. How many families are destroyed due to arguments or anger for just one minute that spoiled a lifetime of happiness and love?

Before I go any further just to let you know I am not a very religious man. But I do believe in God. On one of my many near-death experiences I felt like I had died and was floating in the clouds. I could hear my daughter talking, but in the distance; I didn't feel present with her. Luckily the doctors did what they had to do to save me, and I am forever grateful that I was able to survive to write this book.

I believe it must be in my DNA. I have always been a person who tries to help others live a better life. We all know life is not an easy journey. However, if you do it right, in the end you make yourself happy and everyone around you as well. So I believe that in keeping a positive mental attitude, life gets easier. Just give it time.

Remember we only have one lifetime to make the right choices and build good habits. In this wonderful world, we are in charge of our destiny.

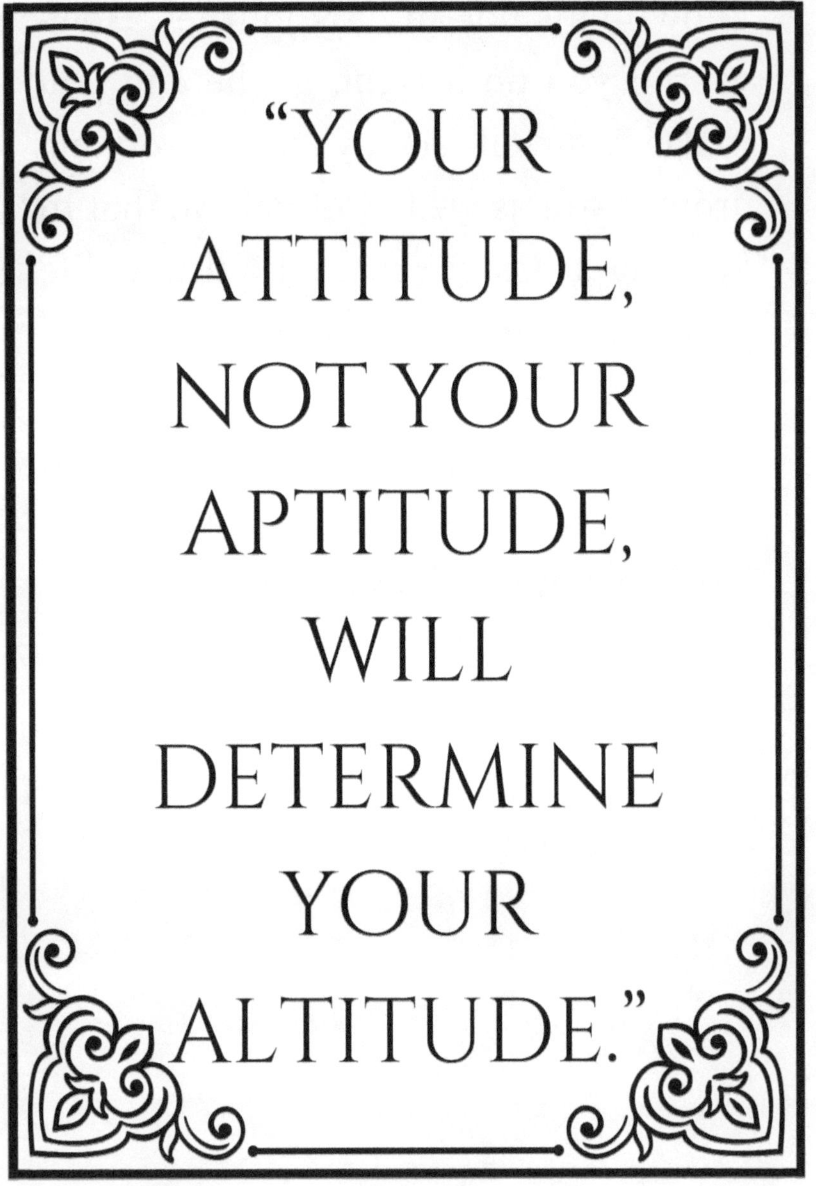

"YOUR ATTITUDE, NOT YOUR APTITUDE, WILL DETERMINE YOUR ALTITUDE."

-Zig Ziglar

15

ALWAYS HAVE A POSITIVE MENTAL ATTITUDE

I believe it is important to find the joy in everything you do, no matter how impossible it may seem. I have had to clean meat trimmings and use a steam hose to chase rats out of elevator shafts, climbed into sewer pits, and done a number of jobs that would qualify as 'the worst jobs ever', but I have always managed to find the good and obtain happiness from them, even joking and laughing about how terrible they were. Sometimes it is from my pride in a job well done, the recognition from my bosses, or simply the relief from knowing something unpleasant has been taken care of. Sometimes my wife is feeling under the weather and so I will do a chore I hate so that she doesn't have to do it. Then I can take joy in the fact that I have taken something off her plate so that she can enjoy some rest!

I do not believe we will ever have a perfect world, or life. This is why I keep repeating that we need to make it the best we can by focusing on all the good this world has to offer. Always keeping a positive mental attitude. If you want to live a happy life, enjoy every minute of each day, no matter what is handed to you. Make your own heaven on earth with your mind. Just in case there is no heaven. It all goes back to you, to create your own destiny by the choices you make and the habits you create.

As I look back at my life, I made many mistakes, but I learned more with each one.

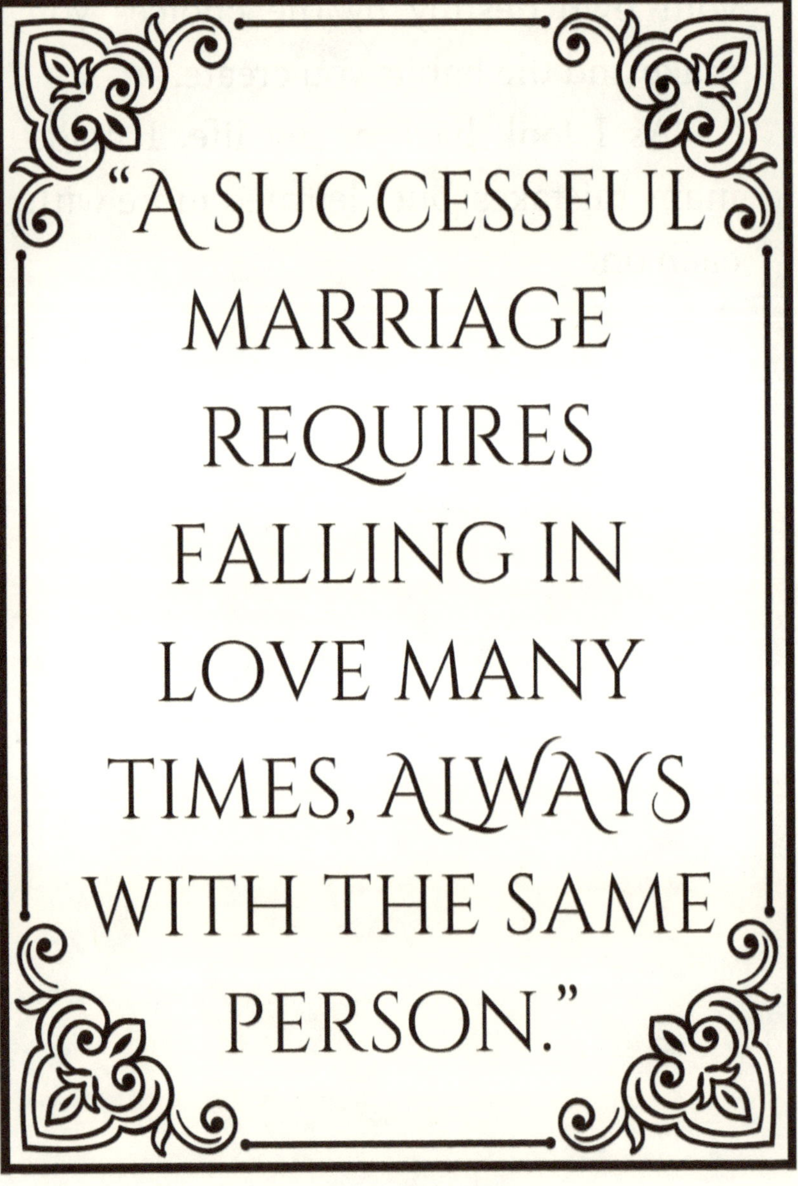

-Mignon McLaughlin

16

WHAT IS THE SECRET TO YOUR MARRIAGE?

Love and appreciation for each other.

Accepting marriage as a 50/50 proposition.

To agree to disagree at times and still love each other.

Never hold a grudge.

Let her do her things and I do mine.

We are all unique. No one is perfect. But if you really love someone, you will accept them the way they are.

"LIKE STARS I AM SURROUNDED BY DARKNESS. LIKE STARS I STILL MANAGE TO SHINE."

DEPRESSION

I could write an entire book on this subject, but revisiting that period of my life is difficult and filled with bad memories, so we will stick to one chapter.

The first thing to mention is that I didn't know I was in a depression. I'd been promoted at work, which came with extra stress and responsibilities, but instead of being able to go home after a long day and relax, I went to the campground, where there were always jobs to do, problems to fix, and not a moment of peace. As if the stress and financial burden of a full-time job and budding business weren't enough, one of my family members had completely lost their way. It terrified me and broke my heart, but the worst part was that I didn't know how to fix it. I couldn't. Which made me feel useless. I was sinking and couldn't claw my way out. By the time I realized how bad it was, the only solution I could see was taking my own life. I was debating between a shotgun to the head or just crashing my car into a tree when nature took care of it for me, and I collapsed with the symptoms of a heart attack.

I spent a week in the intensive care unit, which forced me to slow down, but the lack of jobs to keep me busy just gave me more time to spend with my demons. The more time I was out sick, the more work that would pile up and be waiting for me once I got out. There was no end in sight.

I don't think I admitted to myself, or to anyone else, how severely depressed I was at that time, not until I sat down to write my autobiography and I had to revisit that period in painful detail. Thankfully, someone who was on my team at Pratt and had helped me build an expansion to my residence at the campground, noticed. I would probably have denied it if he'd called me out on it, but instead he gave me a book to motivate me during my recovery, that he said had helped him through a similar situation. It was *The Greatest Secret in the World*, by Og Mandino. I devoured that book, as well as his other works, and tried to live by the Serenity Prayer, though I struggle with that to this day.

If you meet me in person, we can talk for hours about all the books that helped me find my way out, but until then, I've put a list at the end of this book. I am not saying a book can save your life, but then again, I am not saying that it can't. You have to be open to the lessons and willing to put in the time and effort to make the changes. Even a month earlier, I might have left that book on my desk, or read a few pages and forgotten about it, but by the time it was given to me, I was desperate and would have tried anything.

I am someone who likes to always be doing something, to find a solution for every problem, to take care of things now instead of putting it off to tomorrow. I am sure it is very frustrating when I tend to expect the same from the people around me, but it is how I have always been. Unfortunately, I can't control everything, and a lot of my stress was due to things that were out of my control. I would focus on them, to the detriment of things that I could actually fix, and it took those books to remind me what was important, and to help me focus my time and energy. I learnt not to pray for money, love, good health, fame, success, or happiness. Instead, I prayed for guidance, to be shown the way to acquire these things. Our prayers are often answered when we put ourselves on the path to accomplishing them ourselves and are open to receive them.

Barbara and I also took frequent vacations after that point, but unlike our previous trips, where I tried to run

away from problems that inevitably fol-
lowed me, I was able to put my worries
aside, to leave my businesses under the
care of others, and actually trust them
to take care of it rather than stressing
out about it the whole time I was away.
That kind of a vacation, and the effect it
has on your mental health, is priceless.

"WE DON'T STOP PLAYING BECAUSE WE GROW OLD; WE GROW OLD BECAUSE WE STOP PLAYING."
-George Bernard Shaw

18

FAMILY IS EVERYTHING

As so many families grow apart as soon as the children have families of their own, I have often been asked how mine has managed to stay so close? I think the answer is that I treat them the way I like to be treated, with love, kindness, and compassion, and I try my best to be generous. Oh, and to celebrate as many family occasions as I can!

·　·　·

FAMILY COMES in all shapes and sizes. It isn't always the one you were born into, but I was lucky to have the most amazing mother, and a father who, though stern and less affectionate than I would have liked, always supported me, and made sure I had the skills and knowledge to make it in the world. My siblings, Roger, Georges, Irene, and Fay, were not only the children I grew up with, but the best friends I treasured through my adult years. We worked together, vacationed together, raised our kids together, and had dinner together most Tuesday nights. Today there is only me and Fay left, but while she lives far away, we make it a point to stay in touch and see each other multiple times a year. Because family is everything. Losing my parents and most of my siblings has been extremely diffi-cult, but that is where another type of family comes in. The one you make.

At the core of everything is Barbara, my wife of sixty-six years, who makes every house a home, brightens all my days, and without whom I would be nothing. Together, we built a family with three children, six grandchildren, and soon to be seven great-grandchil-dren, making my world the best anyone could ever wish for. When I was younger, working multiple jobs and doing everything I could to support my family and ensure they had every op-portunity and benefit that I never had, I missed out on a lot of things. Sure, my kids would sometimes follow in my morning routine, and we took family vacations, but on a day-to-day basis, my wife was the one holding down the fort and acting as a single parent.

But family was always incredibly important to me. The most important thing, honestly. When we opened our restaurant, Barbara's brother was our executive chef, her father worked in the kitchen, our sisters and my nieces were waitresses, and our kids helped out however they could. Once the campground was my full-time job, we made it the center of family life for all those we cared about.

I know that one of the main reasons I am still alive today is because I rarely go more than a day without a visit from one of them. Every Wednesday, Friday, and Sunday, the whole family is invited, though they are welcome any time. Not everyone comes three times a week, but Sundays are sacred, where we spend the day in the backyard during the summer, or watching the great-grand-children play inside in the winter. It is often loud and chaotic and there are a million things going on at once, but it is without a doubt what has kept me going, through heart attacks, broken backs, multiple forms of cancer, etc. You need to have something to live for, and my family is that for me. I thank God every day that they were all born happy and healthy and am so grateful for every one of them.

LAST, but definitely not least is the family you find along the way. When I married Barbara, she came with five sisters and two brothers who immedi-ately became mine. It is easy to get close to people at work, but it is harder to cultivate those relationships outside the workplace. Luckily, I always had a side project I was working on – usually something I was building – that could benefit from the expertise of my colleagues. Looking to them for help and trusting their skills over a stranger made my life easier, but it also brought new levels to those relationships, and turned colleagues into friends. Then, once we were friends, I included them in weekly dinners, game nights, and parties, which turn friends into family. I think it also helped a lot that I have always had a close family that people actually want to be a part of, so once they are brought in, they never want to leave!

Barbara and I were so used to working with family members, at both the restaurant and the campground, that our family business became more of a family than anything else. Not just because of who we hired, but how we treated them (and the campers who kept coming back, year after year. Some of them even stayed during the winter, so we included them in our holidays, even the big anniversary parties we have now, over a decade after we sold the campground). Our indoor staff would arrive well before their 8 a.m. shift because Barb would have breakfast ready for them. At lunchtime, it wasn't odd to have a dozen people crowded around the table, because all friends and family members (and anyone who didn't prefer to go home to their site) were welcome to have lunch with us. We weren't always there for supper, but if we were, especially on Wednesdays, Fridays, and Sundays, you got a home-cooked family dinner, for which the leftovers would be put in the fridge for anyone who wanted them. We even had our dining room table specially made to accommodate so many people! I don't miss owning the campground with all the headaches it caused, but I definitely miss seeing everyone I love on a daily basis, and having a crowded table for every meal.

I am so blessed to have my children and grandchildren so close. Even their friends and in-laws have found their way in! From my daughter's friend who came on our family vacations and worked for us, to my granddaughter's best friend who did the same and became our seventh grandchild, or even my sister-in-law's nephew (and his wife) who became one of my best friends. One of my oldest friends was someone

I worked with, who became a friend, which introduced his daughter to my son, and made us family.

No matter where it comes from, I hold on to it!

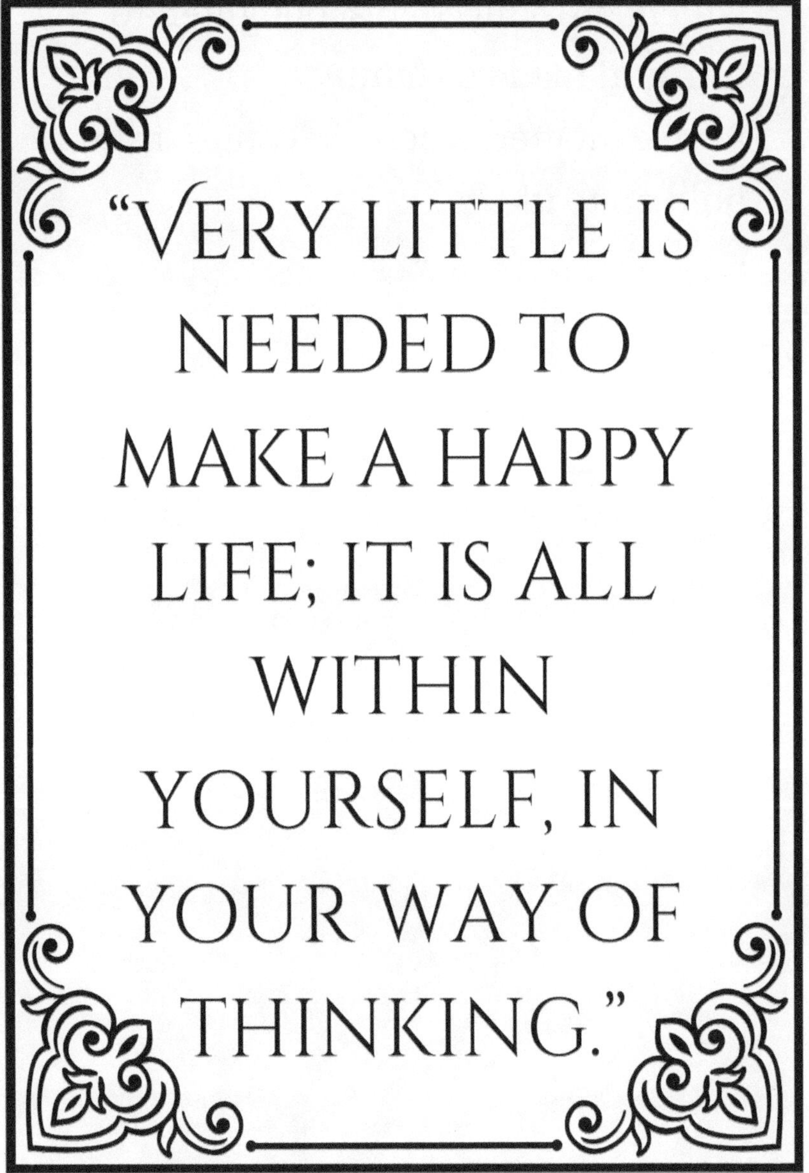

-Marcus Aurelius

19

CHANGE YOUR EXPECTATION FOR APPRECIATION

I believe I created my life. I had many dreams, and am extremely aware of how fortunate I am that they all came true (though not always in the way I expected). I was lucky to drive beautiful cars and motorhomes, and ended up with a beautiful home along a river, facing a mountain. It is a million-dollar view that I appreciate immensely, every minute of every day. Still, there is nothing that I appreciate more than the amazing family I built with my wife, Barbara. This is what makes my life so happy. Like Michael J. Fox said, "Family is not an important thing. It's everything."

I don't think anyone would argue if I said I was a hard worker, especially in my youth. As soon as my daughter was born in 1962, my priorities shifted, and I became a new man with a lot more responsibilities; to keep a roof over our heads and food on the table. This often meant going from a full-time day job to night and weekend jobs, all while running my own business and hoping my wife and children would remember what I looked like. We went on family vacations and spent time at the lake, but some of my holidays were just as stressful as work. (The time the trailer I borrowed fell off a cliff being only one example!)

One thing I hope to do with this book is to inspire people to never give up and always have hope. To dream and think big. But also recognize what you have and be grateful for it. Appreciate it. I was incredibly ambitious and worked my way up through the various companies I was employed at, but there came a point where I had to stop striving for the next milestone and find a way to balance work and family in a way that wouldn't send me to an early grave. Instead of going after another promotion at Pratt & Whitney, I took my retirement.

I can write an entire chapter on my retirement party and how grateful I am for every single person who made it a night I will never forget, but suffice it to say it was the best retirement party in the history of retirement parties.

The hitch is that I didn't actually retire. I transitioned from a senior project manager for a corporation to an entrepreneur with a family business. And while the work was definitely not easy, and I had yet to have my last heart attack, it was with people I loved. I was building a family you could only dream of, where I saw my three children and six grandchildren at least three times a week, if not every single day. I was able to experience all the major milestones in my grandchildren's lives, and get to know them in a way I had been too busy to do with my own children. The campground was my chance to watch my grandchildren grow up, to appre-ciate everything I had worked my whole life for, and I didn't want to miss it.

That's why, less than six months after I retired, when I was offered another job, more prestigious than any I'd held before, I said no. Because I didn't want to be one of those people who doesn't appreciate what they have until it's gone. I wanted to spend every day surrounded by everything and everyone I love. I am the luckiest man in the world, and I appreciate every second of it.

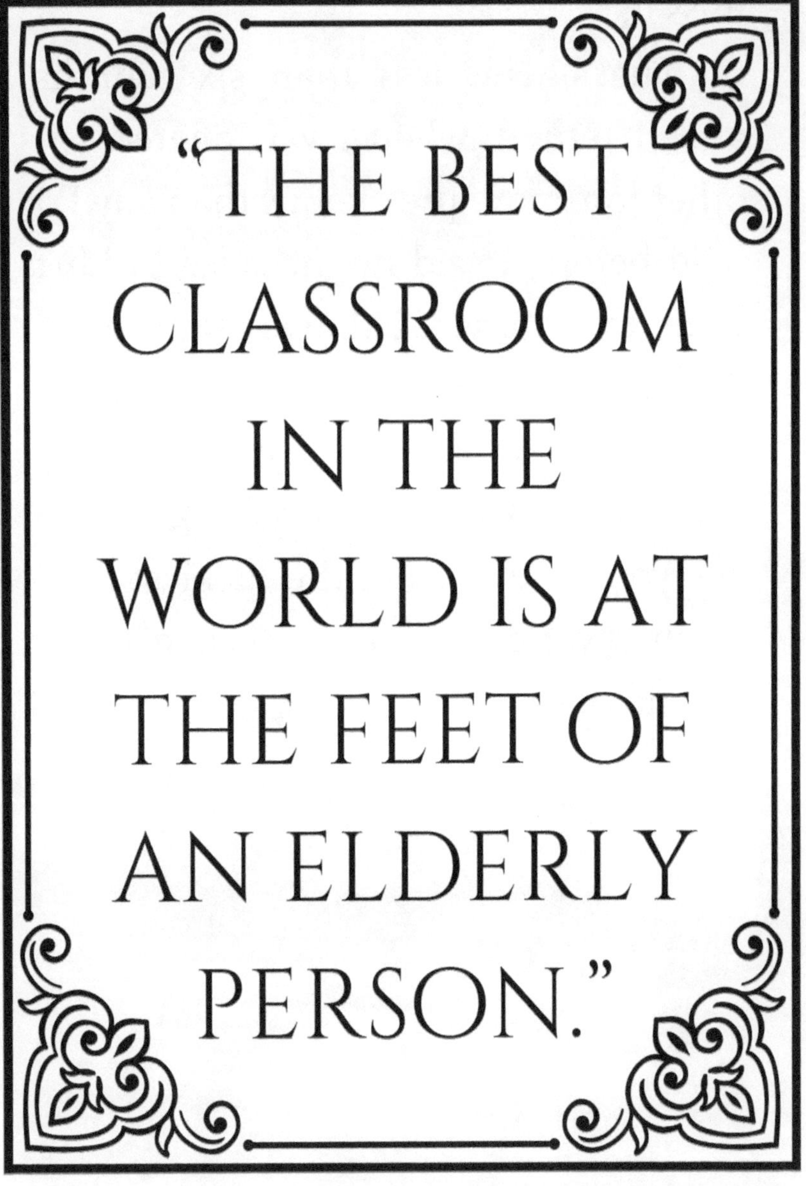
"THE BEST CLASSROOM IN THE WORLD IS AT THE FEET OF AN ELDERLY PERSON."

-Andy Rooney

20

THE WISDOM OF ELDERS

I recently had the honor of speaking with an elderly gentleman and hearing his life story. I was floored, hanging on to every word he said. I used to pride myself on being tough, and while I have mellowed in my old age, I don't think anyone could listen to him without tearing up. I am crying again just thinking of this thirteen-year-old boy who watched his parents get shot in front of him, survived on slivers of bread, and built himself up to a successful businessman.

We often praise people to whom tragedies have occurred, for how resilient they are. We applaud the communities that came together to help those who couldn't help themselves. I am equally in awe of these people and the struggles they go through, the acts of bravery they enact. But it always makes me think about the root of these problems, and how we can try to fix the disease instead of merely dealing with the symptoms. There are natural disasters and unexpected tragedies we can prepare for and deal with as best we can, but there are also wars and gun violence, famine and diseases that could be prevented. I am not going to get into politics, or debate left or right, but I hope we can all agree that human life is precious, and it doesn't make sense to see all the children in war-torn countries dying in bombings or from starvation, becoming orphans, living without basic human rights, or decency. Even in our own countries, where we are supposed to be living the (North) American dream, there are so many senseless deaths happening every day.

One of the reasons humans study history is supposed to be so that we don't repeat our mistakes, but I think we are missing the mark. I was very young during the Second World War, and thankfully don't remember it like that gentleman does, but I always wondered how they let such horrible things happen. How you could see the atrocities being committed and not do every-thing in your power to stop them? Unfortunately, we are in a similar situa-tion today, watching horrific news re-ports and I – like those people I judged – am letting it happen. Because I don't know what else to do, other than vote in someone with the power to change things, to make the right decisions, that I can look up to as a leader.

But how can one person make a dif-ference? Well, one person can become a couple, a few turns into a group, and when all our voices are heard together, we are impossible to ignore. That is why I am writing this book and spreading my message, in the hopes that one day we can have peace on earth, but with the knowledge that it begins at home, with me...and you.

"Never doubt that a small group of
thoughtful, committed citizens can
change the world; indeed, it's the only
thing that ever has."
-Margaret Mead

AFTERWORD

This is the third book that I have written and published, all in the hopes of inspiring people to believe in themselves. If this book has inspired you and you want to know more details about my life and my amazing family you can get *Unbelievable but True* wherever books are sold.

The purpose in life is to have a purpose. My greatest achievement in life was not winning awards or earning money, but doing something I believe is worthwhile; to make our wonderful world a better place. Words are all I have. I hope that my experiences and the wisdom that helped me will help others.

AUTHORS THAT HAVE INSPIRED ME

Og Mandino (The Greatest Secret in the World)

Napoleon Hill (Think and Grow Rich)

Dale Carnegie (How to Win Friends and Influence People)

Denis Waitley (Seeds of Greatness)

Norman Vincent Peale (The Power of Positive Thinking)

Russell H. Conwell (Acres of Diamonds)

Louise Aronson (Elderhood)

Barack Obama

Michelle Obama

www.ingramcontent.com/pod-product-compliance
Lightning Source LLC
Chambersburg PA
CBHW022103050726
47591CB00002B/648